THEMATIC UNIT
SEASONS

Written by Ireta Sitts Graube

Teacher Created Materials, Inc.
6421 Industry Way
Westminster, CA 92683
www.teachercreated.com
©1990 Teacher Created Materials, Inc.
Revised 1998, Reprinted, 2001
Made in U.S.A.
ISBN-1-55734-251-1

Illustrated by
Blanca Apodaca
Edited by
*Ina Massler Levin, M.A. and
Janet Cain, M.Ed.*

Table of Contents

Introduction

Seasons contains four captivating, whole language, mini-thematic units. Its 80 exciting pages are filled with a wide variety of lesson ideas and reproducible pages designed for use with early childhood students. At its core are four high-quality children's literature selections, *The Seasons of Arnold's Apple Tree, The Snowy Day, My Spring Robin,* and *Time of Wonder.* For each of these books, activities are included that set the stage for reading, encourage the enjoyment of the book, and extend the concepts gained. In addition, the theme is connected to the curriculum with activities in language arts (including language experience and writing suggestions), math, science, social studies, art, music, and life skills (cooking, physical education, etc.). Many of these activities encourage cooperative learning. Suggestions and patterns for bulletin boards are additional time savers for the busy teacher. Furthermore, directions for student-created big books and a culminating activity, which allow students to synthesize their knowledge in order to create products that can be shared beyond the classroom, highlight this very complete teacher resource.

This thematic unit includes:

☐ **literature selections** — summaries of four books with related lessons and reproducible pages that cross the curriculum

☐ **poetry and drama** — suggested selections and lessons enabling students to compose their own poetry and act out and create their own stories

☐ **language experience and writing ideas** — suggestions for daily writing activities across the curriculum, including making books

☐ **bulletin board ideas** — suggestions and plans for student-created and/or interactive bulletin boards

☐ **curriculum connections** — activities in language arts, science, math, social studies, art, music, and life skills such as cooking and physical education

☐ **group projects** — to encourage cooperative learning

☐ **culminating activities** — which require students to synthesize their learning and create products that can be shared with others

☐ **a bibliography** — suggested additional fiction and nonfiction books, poetry, and technology resources

---

To keep this valuable resource intact so it can be used year after year, you may wish to punch holes in the pages and store them in a three-ring binder.

Introduction *(cont.)*

Why Whole Language?

A whole language approach involves children in using all modes of communication: reading, writing, listening, observing, illustrating, experiencing, and doing. Communication skills are interconnected and integrated into lessons that emphasize the whole of language rather than isolating its parts. The lessons revolve around selected literature. Reading is not taught as a separate subject from writing and spelling, for example. A child reads, writes (spelling appropriately for his/her level), speaks, listens, etc. in response to a literature experience introduced by the teacher. In this way, language skills grow naturally, stimulated by involvement and interest in the topic at hand.

Why Thematic Planning?

One very useful tool for implementing an integrated whole language program is thematic planning. By choosing a theme with correlating literature selections for a unit of study, a teacher can plan activities throughout the day that lead to a cohesive, in-depth study of the topic. Students will be practicing and applying their skills in meaningful contexts. Consequently, they will tend to learn and retain more. Both teachers and students will be freed from a day that is broken into unrelated segments of isolated drill and practice.

Why Cooperative Learning?

Besides academic skills and content, students need to learn social skills. No longer can this area of development be taken for granted. Students must learn to work cooperatively in groups in order to function well in modern society. Group activities should be a regular part of school life and teachers should consciously include social objectives as well as academic objectives in their planning. For example, a group working together to write a report may need to select a leader. The teacher should make clear to the students and monitor the qualities of good leader-follower group interaction just as he/she would state and monitor the academic goals of the project.

Why Big Books?

An excellent cooperative, whole language activity is the production of Big Books. Groups of students, or the whole class, can apply their language skills, content knowledge, and creativity to produce a Big Book that can become a part of the classroom library to be read and reread. These books make excellent culminating projects for sharing beyond the classroom with parents, librarians, other classes, etc. Big Books can be produced in many ways and this thematic unit book includes directions for at least one method you may choose.

Seasons

Seasons is a set of four thematic teaching units that involve children in all modes of learning. There is a wealth of books dealing with seasons for the child and the teacher. Most of these will need to be read by the teacher to the student, but some are suitable for the beginning reader. See the Bibliography on page 80 for many suggestions.

Activities for All Seasons

The activities the child can experience to learn about seasons are many and varied. Writing Big Books to tell about the current, following, or preceding season is always fun. Taking a listening walk to hear the sounds of the season or visiting an adopted tree and noting the changes each season, use all the child's senses to enhance the learning process. Graphing the weather changes during each season and calculating how many days each season will last, help the child discover problem solving techniques. Using all small motor skills when making and illustrating seasonal art projects will add to the child's knowledge of the seasons.

The Seasons of Arnold's Apple Tree

by Gall Gibbons

Summary

Arnold watches his tree grow buds in the spring. He builds a swing in it and weaves an apple-blossom wreath. The summer finds Arnold in his tree building a tree house and shading himself from the sun and the summer showers. The apples are green now, and Arnold can juggle them. In the fall the apples are red and the leaves have turned golden and are drifting to the ground. Arnold plays in the fallen leaves and collects apples to take home. His family makes apple pie and apple cider. Next, winter arrives and snow falls on Arnold's bare tree. He hangs popcorn and berries on its branches for the birds. Arnold builds a snow fort and a snowman to keep him and his tree company. Then the snow melts and it's spring again.

This book makes an excellent introduction to the study of the seasons since it covers the complete year. The activities for this section are written so they may be used in the fall; however, the book is suitable for use at any time during the school year.

SETTING THE STAGE

Science Center

Materials: Pieces of bark; various sizes, shapes, and colors of leaves; apples of various color and sizes; scissors

Directions: The children examine the items, make leaf prints or trace around the leaves. They compare colors and sizes of apples. Later these apples can be cut up and the taste and texture compared.

SETTING THE STAGE *(cont.)*

Bulletin Board

Objective: This bulletin board allows students to participate in decorating a tree to match the season.

Materials: Blue or black butcher paper for background; dark brown butcher paper for tree; pins or staples; sign (page 8); scissors; colored construction paper for apples and leaves

Construction: Cut a rectangle 1/4 the width of your bulletin board for the trunk. Cut shorter, thinner strips for the branches. Wrinkle and crush the butcher paper to give the effect of bark. Twist branches and turn the paper as you pin it on the board to give a 3-D effect. The trunk can fit on your bulletin board or it can extend down to the floor. Add the sign on the next page, enlarged or as is.

Directions: After reading *Arnold's Apple Tree*, have students prepare leaves and apples to match the season under discussion.

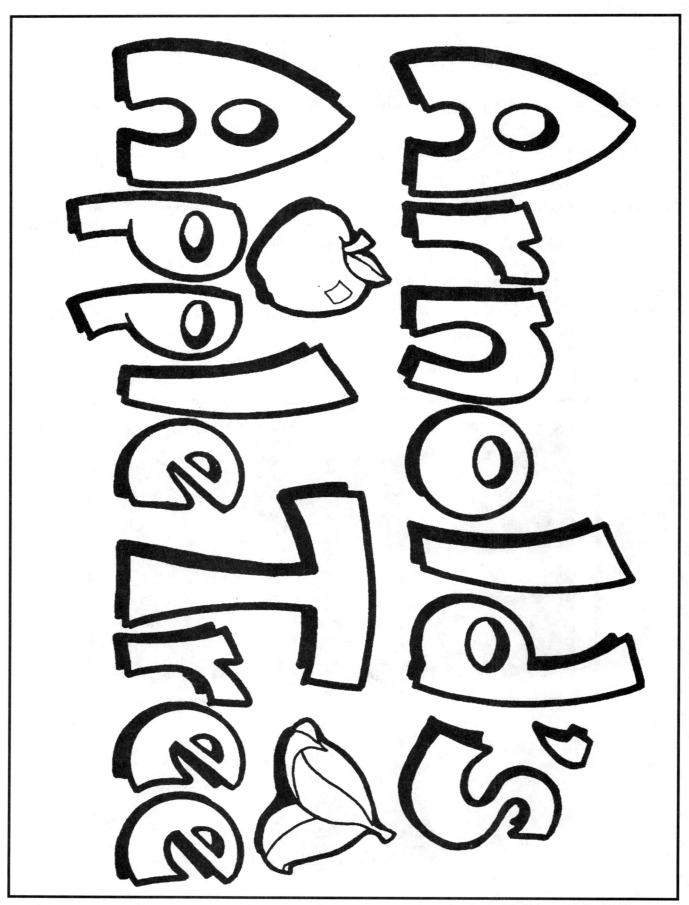

8

ENJOYING THE BOOK

Season Order

Read the book to the class. Discuss the seasons in the book and write on the chalkboard the order in which they are presented. Ask the children to tell you what season it is right now. Write down the order of the seasons as they will experience them in school.

Compare the two lists.

Spring	**Fall**
Summer	**Winter**
Fall	**Spring**
Winter	**Summer**

Reread the section on fall. List on a chart or chalkboard what happened to the tree in the fall. What did Arnold's family make from apples? What else did he make from apples for Halloween?

Leaf Messages

The child traces around an apple leaf pattern (page 10) or draws one free-hand. (The teacher may wish to have duplicates of page 10 for the children to cut and use as needed.) The child tells something about fall and the teacher records it on the leaf. The child places leaf on bulletin board tree or on a real branch that has been placed in a corner of the classroom. (Place branch of tree in bucket that has been filled with sand or dirt.)

The children may also put (or hide) apple leaf messages around the classroom. They can dictate their message to the teacher to record. These might be messages to remind the class to go to recess at a certain time, to record the weather each day, or to water the plants. They might also be personal messages written to one child or the class, or the teacher. Children love making these and finding them!

Apple Leaf Patterns

* See suggested uses, page 9.

Big and Little Books

Using Big and Little Books

Reading readiness is promoted when children participate in the production of a Big Book so that they become very familiar with its text. Then, children may make a matching little book. Now, they have their own book that they can "read" all by themselves.

Big Book

Make a class book. This will be a fall leaves book. Ask the children what happens to the leaves on a tree in the fall. Guide the children to tell you what colors the leaves turn. Elicit the sentences on the little book pages (see pages 13 and 14). Write each sentence on a separate large sheet of paper. ("The leaves turn yellow" "The leaves turn red." etc.) This can be written on a chart and then recopied onto separate pages for the Big Book or written on separate sheets of paper as the children dictate. Groups of children may work together to illustrate each page. Then it should be bound into a Big Book.

Little Book

To make the Little Book, copy pages 13 and 14 back-to-back, one for each child. Cut the page in half and staple it together, making sure you have "Fall Leaves" as the cover. You will have eight pages, counting the title page. Because the words are repeated so often in this story, some children will be able to read it right away and others will memorize it. After the children have finished illustrating the book, they can work with a partner "reading" the book. They can also "read" it to an older child, parent volunteer, aide, or the teacher. Children may take the small books home to keep. A sample letter to parents about little books is on page 12.

Taking Big Books Home

Checking out Big Books to take home for one night is simple if the children can do it themselves. Place each Big Book in a plastic bag with a handle. These can be ordered from supply stores. (See Bibliography, page 80 for source.) Use clear contact paper to fasten a note to parents (page 12) inside the bag.

Make a check out poster with library pockets. On the library pocket make a sketch of the book and write the title. Make it the same color as the book cover. This will help children who are not reading to check out the book they want. Children place a laminated name card in the pocket for the book they are taking.

Parent Letters About Books

Teacher Directions: Send the top letter with the first Little Book you send home. Attach the note at the bottom with clear contact paper to the bags that contain the Big Books.

Dear Parents,

Today your child is bringing home a Little Book. This is just one of many your child will receive this year.

The Little Books are miniatures of the books, poems, or charts that we look at in our classroom. These books are for you to enjoy with your child. Let your child "read" the book to you. Don't worry if your child doesn't have all the right words or if he or she is memorizing the text. This is how reading starts. Celebrate what your child can do and the interest shown in wanting to learn to read.

Thank you for taking the time to share these little books. Your involvement is critical to your child's success.

Sincerely,

_____

Teacher

Dear Parents,

I am bringing this BIG BOOK home to read to you. Please take time to listen to me read it and help me to remember to return it to school tomorrow.

Thank you.

This book
was
illustrated
by

_____
Name

fold

8

cut   here

Fall Leaves

1

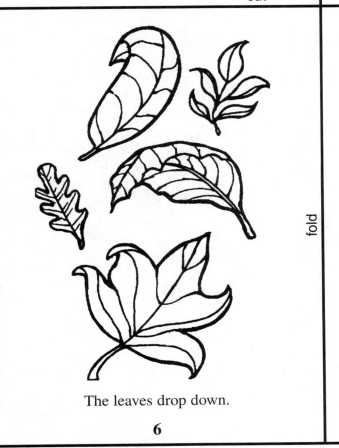

fold

The leaves drop down.

6

The leaves turn red.

3

The leaves turn yellow.

2

fold

cut

The End

here

7

The leaves drop orange.

4

fold

The leaves turn brown.

5

EXTENDING THE BOOK

Daily Writing

Children cut pictures of different seasons out of magazines. Teacher labels and places them in class book or on bulletin board. Children can match the names of season labels with pictures or write name of season. The teacher will need to help those children not ready to write themselves.

Children can tell older students, aides, or parent volunteers about the current season and what they like to do outside during it. The older person will record and read it to the class. These can be compiled into Big Books, posted on bulletin boards, or kept in a class notebook.

Have the children describe the current season. The teacher records the words or sentences on chart paper or chalkboard. The children copy a word or sentence and illustrate it. This may be kept in a seasonal notebook or sent home.

Keep a daily weather journal. See page 16.

Writing Challenges

Use these writing ideas to challenge able students:

Keep a daily log of your trip to school. What signs of the season did you see?

Write all the words that remind you of the current season.

What season does your pet like best and why?

If you have no pet, what pet would like the current season and why?

If you were a fish, would you know what season it was? If so how, and if not, why not?

What season were you born in? Ask your parents to describe your birthday. Write it | down.

Name _____

Weather Journal

_____
date

Today is _____
day of week

sunny

cloudy

rainy

windy

snowy

foggy

Today it is _____.

Squirrel Math

Materials: for each student—one copy of this page, ten nuts, nut cup, crayons

Directions: After coloring, children use Sammy Squirrel and the nuts to help them illustrate problems. For example: Sammy Squirrel has five nuts. (Put nuts in Sammy's hands.) He eats two nuts. (Move nuts to Sammy's mouth.) How many nuts are left?

Math

Weighing Apples

Have each child bring an apple to school. Weigh the apples on a food scale to see how much each weighs. Discuss units of measure.

Math Center Activity — Have a balance scale available and objects for comparison of weights. Example: apples and paper clips.

Apple Graph

Materials: White butcher paper or chart paper; 3 x 3 inch (8 x 8 cm) squares of white paper or sticky notes (one per child); crayons; glue; apples which children have brought to school

Directions: Put the title "Apple Graph" at the top of the paper. Make three columns and label them: Green, Red, Yellow. Display the graph so children can reach it.

Using the paper squares, the children draw an apple and color it the same color as the apple they brought to school. Each child glues their apple picture in the correct column. Which column has the most, the least?

Apple Math Concentration

Materials: Apple sheet (page 19); red tagboard or red construction paper; felt pen; scissors

Preparation: Make four copies of the apple card sheet (page 19) on white paper. Paste them onto red tagboard or construction paper. Laminate and cut out. Write matching numbers or equations on the white sides of pairs of apples, except the apples with a worm.

Directions: Two to four children can play the game. Turn all apples face down. Take turns finding matching pairs and saying the name of the number or the answer to the equation. When a child finds a pair, he keeps it. If a child turns over one worm and one number, he loses a turn. If he gets matching worms, he gets an extra turn. The child with the most pairs wins the game.

Variations: This game can be used for shape recognition, letters, words, sounds, etc.

Additional Math Activities

Estimate the total number of apples in a group. Then count to check.

Teacher cuts an apple to discuss halves and fourths.

Cut an apple for each child. Students remove the seeds from their apples and count them. Glue the seeds to another sheet of paper and draw an apple around them. Write the number of seeds.

An excellent way for children to practice following directions and learn about measurement is to cook. Have them make applesauce or baked apples. Recipes can be found in many cookbooks.

Apple Math Concentration Cards

Art and Dramatic Play

Sponge Painted Trees

Materials: Sponges; tempera paints (orange, yellow, red, green, and brown); foam meat trays or containers; light blue construction paper; brown crayons; tagboard; tree pattern, (page 21)

Preparation: Using the pattern on page 21, make a stencil from tagboard. Cut small sponges into fourths.

Directions: Using a brown crayon, trace tree pattern onto light blue construction paper. Sponge paint the tree trunk in brown. Let dry. Sponge paint leaves onto the branches of the tree using orange, red, and yellow paint. Sponge paint green grass.

Leaf Art

Materials: Several one inch (2.5 cm) squares of red and orange tissue paper and a few green squares (for each child); black construction paper; glue; chalk

Directions: The child draws a leaf on the black construction paper with chalk. The tissue paper squares are glued down on top to make a collage.

(This same technique can be used to make an apple, pumpkin, or squirrel.)

Dramatic Play

I SEE THREE

I see three—one, two, three,
Three little cats
Wearing hats.

I see three—one, two, three
Three little frogs
Squatting on logs.

I see three—one, two, three
Three little bears
Without any cares.

I see three—one, two, three
Three little birds
Learning new words.

I see three—one, two, three
Three little bees
Flying up apple trees.

Use this as a fingerplay, holding up one finger at a time, or use it as dramatic play. In acting out this poem, the children can use props or just act like the animals. If you want to use props, make copies of the pictures on pages 22 and 23. Make your own numbers. Color, laminate, and tape the pictures and numbers to craft sticks. Choose children for the various parts and let them act out the poem or hold up their prop. Choose three children to hold up the 1,2,3, signs. If the children are reading, use number words instead.

This can also be used as a flannelboard story. The patterns on pages 22 and 23 can be copied onto paper and colored. Attach a piece of interfacing or flannel to the back. (Or, trace directly onto interfacing or felt.)

Tree Pattern

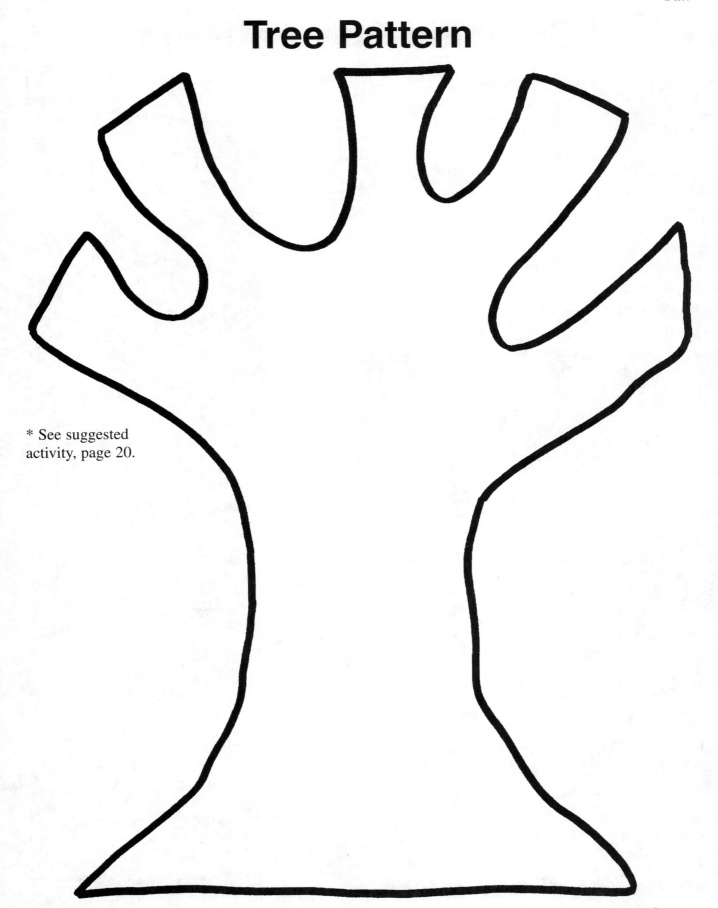

* See suggested activity, page 20.

Dramatic Play Patterns

* See suggested activity, page 20.

Dramatic Play Patterns *(cont.)*

* See suggested activity, page 20.

Science

Adopt a Tree

The class chooses a tree on the school grounds or in the neighborhood to adopt for the school year. Visit the tree in September and then once a month. A large wall chart can be kept in the classroom. Decorate the chart with a tree. The children dictate to the teacher how the tree looks from month to month.

The children can also make a book telling about their tree. Fold a large piece of construction paper in half. The child draws a picture of the tree on the front page. On the second page the child draws a picture of what they would like to do in the tree. On the third page the child draws a picture of how the tree makes him or her feel. The child may write or dictate words for each page. The final page shows how the tree will look during the next season.

Our Tree

Sept.	Oct.	Nov.
Dec.	Jan.	Feb.
March	April	May

Leaf Comparisons

Materials: Leaves from various trees (some that have fallen and some living); magnifying glasses; newsprint; masking tape; peeled crayons or colored chalk (brown, orange, red, yellow, and green)

Directions: Have children find two leaves from the same type of tree, one fallen and one living. Have them examine the leaves under a magnifying glass, naming the things that are the same and different about each leaf. The teacher lists the differences on a science chart to post over the science table.

Tape a leaf to the tabletop. Place a sheet of newsprint on top of it. Show the children how to rub the side of a crayon or chalk over the newsprint until a leaf appears on the paper. Then have the child make a rubbing of a leaf from a different tree and compare the two. Play a game with the rubbings and have children try to identify which rubbings are of the same leaf. Place all the rubbings that have the same shape in one pile. The leaves can also be cut out and placed on the bulletin board tree.

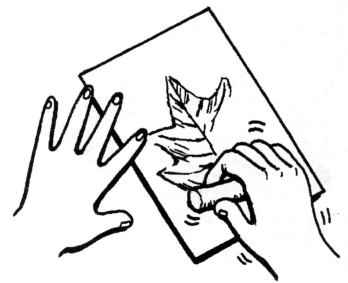

The Snowy Day

by Ezra Jack Keats

Summary

One winter day, Peter wakes up to discover that it has snowed. He jumps into his snowsuit and heads out the door. He has a day full of exciting adventures which include making footprints in the snow, knocking snow off the limbs of a tree, getting in the middle of a snowball fight, making a snowman and a snow angel, and pretending to be a mountain climber. When Peter goes to sleep that night, he dreams that all the snow melts away. However, the next morning he is delighted to find that the snow is still there and new flakes are falling.

This classic is a perfect choice for introducing winter. Its simple story is told with pictures and text that children will enjoy again and again.

SETTING THE STAGE

Discussion

Point out that people and animals store up food to prepare for winter. In many places, it is too cold in the winter to grow food. During the warmer months, some people can freeze vegetables and fruits from their gardens and later are able to enjoy these foods in the winter. Some animals also have ways to store food. Squirrels hide nuts and acorns in tree holes and under the ground so they will have food for the winter. Bears eat large amounts during the fall so they can hibernate, or sleep, during the winter. Chipmunks, groundhogs, snakes, turtles, and frogs also hibernate. Many birds migrate or fly south to find food in warmer climates during the winter months and return in the spring.

Plastic Snowflakes

Materials: Plastic berry basket for each child; scissors; glue; wax paper; glitter; string or thread

Directions: Cut a circular or square shape from the bottom of the plastic berry basket for the snowflake. Place the snowflake on a sheet of wax paper. Cover one side of the snowflake with glue. Sprinkle glitter on it and allow to dry. Carefully turn over the snowflake. Cover the other side with glue and glitter. After the glue dries, gently shake off any excess glitter. Save and reuse the glitter that falls onto the wax paper. Tie a piece of string or thread to the snowflake, and hang it in the window.

Variations:

1. Use the snowflakes as a template for printing snowflake designs. Dip the snowflake in paint and press it onto paper.

2. Use the plastic snowflake pattern as a stencil. Place two or three snowflake stencils on white paper and use black spray paint to cover the paper and snowflakes. Allow the paint to dry. When you remove the snowflake stencils, they will appear white on a black background and look like snowflakes falling at night.

SETTING THE STAGE

Snowman

Materials: 1 cup (250 mL) soap flakes; 1 tablespoon (15 mL) water; bowl; cloves; toothpicks

Directions: Measure and pour the soap flakes into a bowl. Use your hands to mix the water with the soap flakes. Make two ball shapes, one large and one small, from the soap flakes. When the soap balls are firm, use toothpicks to connect them into a snowman shape. Poke cloves into the small soap ball to make the eyes and mouth of the snowman. Poke some cloves into the large soap ball to make buttons down the front.

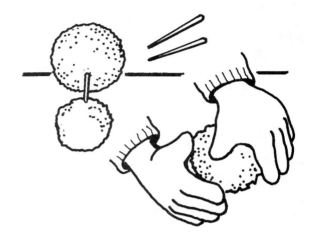

Variations:

1. Use scraps of construction paper or fabric to make clothing, such as a hat, scarf, and mittens, for the snowman.
2. Draw a snowman on white construction paper. Use marker to color details, such as the eyes, nose, mouth, buttons, and a scarf, on the snowman. Prepare a mixture made from equal parts of Epsom salts and warm water. Paint the snowman with the mixture. Allow the picture to dry so sparkly crystals will form. Display the snowman on a bulletin board.

Idea Web

Draw an idea web on the chalkboard or a chart tablet as shown in the following example. Write *Winter Activities* inside the circle. Ask the children to brainstorm a list of activities that they like to do in the winter. Write their suggestions in the ovals.

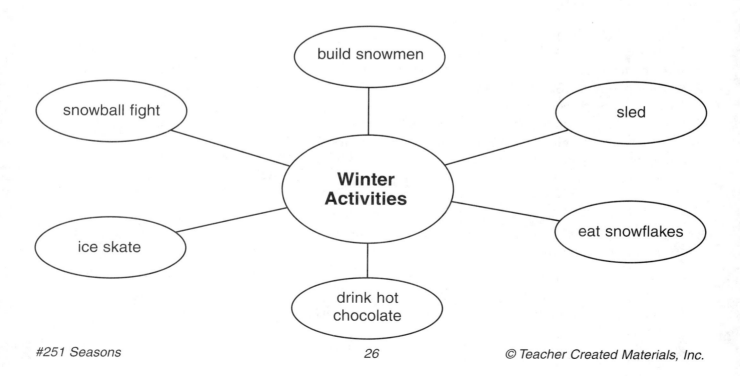

SETTING THE STAGE *(cont.)*

Clothing Game

Materials: 3 bags or boxes; pictures of seasons; felt pen; seasonal clothing for each bag

Preparation: Label each bag with the seasons–fall, winter, spring. If possible, find pictures of each season and paste on the bag below the words. In the fall bag put items appropriate for that season: light jacket, sweater, muffler or scarf. In the winter bag: snow boots, mittens, cap, and coat; in the spring bag place rain boots, rain hat, and raincoat.

Directions: Divide the class into three teams for a relay race. Each child must run to a bag, put on clothes, take them off, and tag the next member of the team. The first team to finish is the winner.

Variations:

1. Let the teams trade bags and try on clothes from another season.
2. Limit the game to only two bags of clothing.
3. Let the children decide what type of clothing belongs in each season and place it in the correct bag.
4. The bags can be placed in the dramatic play center and the children can play dress-up.
5. Discuss what type of clothing is appropriate in your part of the country.

ENJOYING THE BOOK

Mittens

Materials: Patterns on page 29; different colored construction paper; scissors; hole punch; one 12" (30 cm) piece of yarn per child; crayons

Directions: Reproduce the mitten patterns on various colors of construction paper. Have each child decorate a pair of mittens. Emphasize making matching patterns on both mittens. This is a good opportunity to discuss patterns. If the children have a difficult time understanding what to do, create some examples to show them. Each child then colors and cuts out his or her mittens. Punch a hole in the bottom of each mitten, and use yarn to tie them together. Display them on a bulletin board.

Variations:

1. Cut ten mitten shapes from each of two different colors of tagboard, using the pattern on page 29. Write the numerals 1–10 on one set and the corresponding number words on the other set. Have the children sequence the numbers and match the pairs. You may wish to have them count out the correct number of white cotton ball "snowballs" onto the mittens.

2. Cut two sets of 26 mittens (page 29) from two colors of tagboard. Write uppercase letters on one set and lowercase letters on the other set. Ask students to arrange the mittens in alphabetical order and match the uppercase and lowercase letters.

3. Make a set of mittens (page 29) for students to match rhyming words or the beginning sounds of picture names.

4. Reproduce the mitten patterns (page 29) on various colors of construction paper. Be sure all the mittens are facing the same direction. Invite each child to dictate a response to "Winter is the best time for _____." Write each sentence on a mitten. Punch a hole in the bottom of each mitten. Create a class book fastening the mittens together with a metal ring or yarn.

5. Reread *The Snowy Day.* Enlarge the mitten patterns (page 29) to create a class big book. Ask the children to tell about winter adventures they have had. Write their stories on the enlarged mitten patterns.

Winter Walk

Take your class on a winter walk. Encourage the children to touch different parts of the school building. Ask them how different materials, such as metal, brick, glass, and wood, feel. Have them touch other things around the school, such as the bark of trees, dirt, grass, and cement. When you return to the classroom, invite the children to name the things they touched as you list them on the chalkboard.

Mitten Patterns

* See suggested activity, page 28.

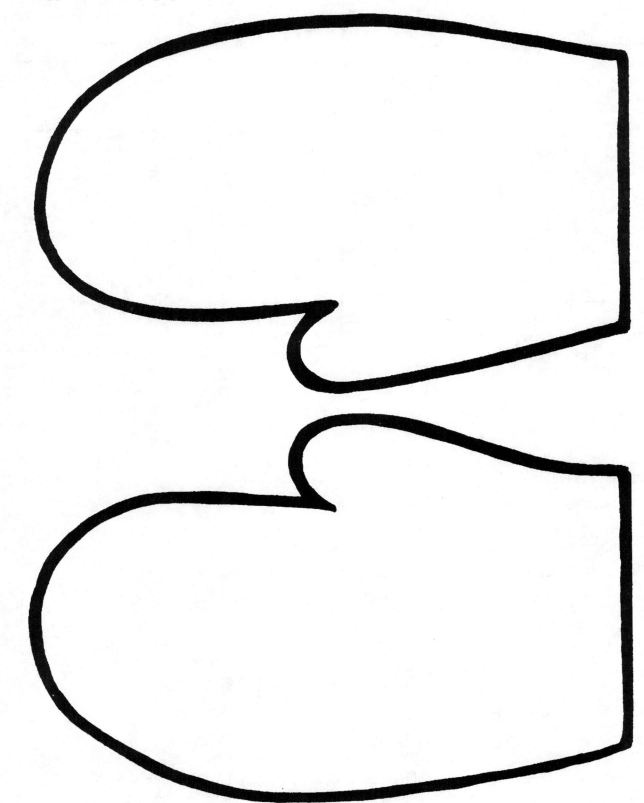

EXTENDING THE BOOK

Winter Pop-Up Book

Materials: White construction paper (one per child); crayons; scissors; pencil; index cards

Preparation: Make a pop-up book with one page per student. For a large class you may wish to put the pages into two books. Measurements are given for 8 1/2 x 11" (21 x 28 cm) paper, but other sizes may be used.

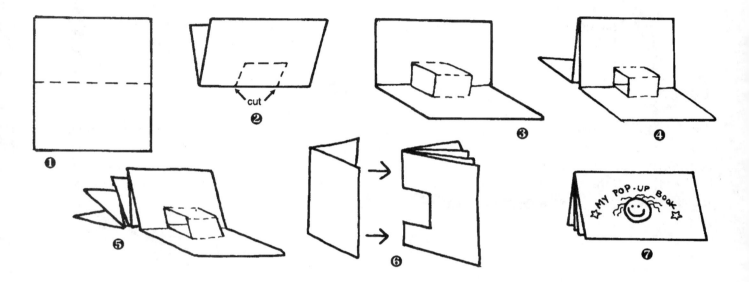

Directions:

1. Fold paper in half crosswise.

2. Measure and mark 2¾" (7 cm) from each side along the fold. Cut 2¾" (7 cm) slits at marks.

3. Push cut area inside out and crease to form pop-up section.

4. Have child draw, color, or cut out something that reminds him of winter. Glue to pop-up portion of the book. Child may name the picture and copy it onto page.

5. Glue two pages back-to-back making sure pop-up section is free.

6. Glue additional pages together until you have a pop-up page for each student.

7. Glue a cover over entire book, and add a title.

Winter Picture Matching

Materials: Magazines; index cards

The children cut winter pictures (for example, snow, ice skates) out of magazines. The teacher writes the words that match the pictures on the index cards. Children match the correct word to the pictures. The pictures and words can be put on the bulletin board or left in a box for children to match. Children who are ready to copy these cards can do so on sentence strips or additional index cards.

EXTENDING THE BOOK *(cont.)*

Snowman Color Hats

Materials: Large dark blue construction paper; orange, red, blue, green, yellow, purple, and black construction paper; white chalk; hat pattern (below); tagboard or cardboard

Directions: Have each child use white chalk to draw a snowman without a hat on large dark blue construction paper. Use the pattern below to make several hats out of tagboard. Let the children trace around the hats on colored construction paper. Each child cuts out one or more hats and labels it with the correct color word. The color words can be copied from the chalkboard or a chart with matching pieces of construction paper beside each word. When finished, the children can place the various hats on the snowmen's heads. They will have fun trading hats with friends.

Variation

After a child cuts out the colored hat, she/he pastes it onto a white piece of construction paper and cuts around it. Now the hat is a color on one side and white on the other side. On the white side, copy the appropriate color word. The child can practice reading color words. If unsure of the word, simply turn it over to find out the color. Play a game with a partner. The person who can read the color word keeps the hat. The person with the most hats at the end of the game is the winner.

Writing Activities

W Is For...

On a chart or on the chalkboard write the names of all the children in the class that have the W for winter in their first or last names. Ask, "How many do we have? Can we make up winter sentences about them?" For instance, "Wendy went walking on an icy day," or, "Max Williams whistled as he skied."

These sentences can be copied and illustrated by children needing a challenge or the teacher can write the sentence on a sheet of paper for the children to illustrate.

Wayne went sledding.

Wendy went walking.

Writing Challenges

These questions can be discussion questions or writing topics. If the child is unable to write the story alone, it can be dictated to the teacher, parent helper, or older student.

If you were an Alaskan Huskie, what would be your favorite season? Why?

What would happen if it never snowed again?

What clothes do you need to play in the snow?

It's winter, and you are picked up by a strong wind and carried away into the sky. What happens to you? Where do you land?

The snow has buried your front door. You can't get out of the house. What will you do?

The winter snow has closed the schools for the day. What will you do?

Math Activities

Snowsuit Story Problems

Materials: A copy of page 34 for each child; ten to twelve cotton balls per child

Preparation: Give each child a copy of page 34. Let them color and paste it onto construction paper.

Directions: Give each child a set of cotton balls. Tell story problems. Have students move cotton ball "snowflakes" onto picture. For example, "Two snowflakes fell and then one more snowflake fell. How many snowflakes fell in all?" Or, have the children pile five snowflakes at the foot of the child. "The child kicked two snowballs away. How many were left?"

Snowflake Math Bingo

Materials: Reproduce playing cards on page 35. You will need one card for each player. Make calling cards with numbers 1-20 for yourself. Each child will need cottonballs or white buttons for snow markers.

Directions: Give each child a Snowflake Math Bingo card and markers. The teacher calls out a number, and the children mark their cards. When they have a row going up and down, across, or on a diagonal, they call out "Snowflake Bingo!" The child who calls out is the winner!

Variations:

Make Snowflake Math Bingo cards with addition or subtraction problems. For children learning one-to-one correspondence, use sets and number matching. This game can also be adapted for reading readiness by using alphabet or sound matching.

Snowsuit Story Problems

* See page 33 for

suggested activity.

Snowflake Bingo ❄

2	7	3	19
9	12	4	15
18	6	13	10
8	16	5	20

Snowflake Bingo ❄

7	14	5	10
15	2	16	6
11	20	8	18
3	9	17	4

Snowflake Bingo ❄

13	9	19	6
5	7	2	15
17	10	20	3
4	8	11	16

Snowflake Bingo ❄

5	17	3	10
9	14	8	16
19	4	18	12
6	20	7	2

Science Activities

Frost Experiment

Materials: Empty metal cans and spoons (one per child); salt; ice cubes; water

Directions: Discuss ice crystals (frost) on windows on a cold morning. Put two to three ice cubes in each can. Cover with water. Add a little salt. Have children stir. (A layer of frost will form on the outside of the can.) Explain that moist air freezes when it touches the sides of the cold can.

Have children touch their nose to the side of the can and repeat:

> **"My nose is as red as a rose**
> **Jack Frost kissed it, I suppose."**

Variation: Write the poem on a sheet of paper and make copies for the children. Let them illustrate it to take home.

Snow Experiment

Materials: Snow or ice; two identical jars; water

Directions: Fill the two jars with snow or ice. Place one in a warm room and one outside in the cold air or in a refrigerator. What happens to each? Why? Set a timer or watch the clock and let a child check the two jars every 15 minutes. Record information on a large sheet of paper.

Variation: Fill one jar with snow or ice and the other with an equal amount of water. Leave them both in a warm room. What happens to the snow? When the snow or ice melts, is there the same amount of water in that jar as in the other one? Why or why not?

Background information for the teacher: Snow is water crystals that have frozen. The crystals freeze when the temperature of the water vapor (as it condenses) is lower than 32°F (0°C). The water vapor expands as it freezes. This means it gets bigger. Snow remains snow only at a certain temperature.

Art Activities

Paper Chain Snowpeople Cooperative Art

Materials: White construction paper strips (1 x 6 inches/2.5 x 15 cm), 11 per child; glue; colored scraps of construction paper or fabrics

Directions: Each child makes a paper chain ten links long. The child then finds a friend and joins their chains together. They find another friend and join these together. This continues until one continuous chain is formed. At this point stop and measure the chain. Spread it out across the classroom. How far does it reach?

Cover a bulletin board with dark background paper. (Black or dark blue butcher paper looks best.) Staple the first link of the chain to the bulletin board, wind the chain around this central point, staple when needed. Continue to form middle and bottom section of snowman. Let children decide what features to add. They can use scrap construction paper or fabric to form mouth, nose, eyes, buttons, scarf, and hat.

Additional Activities: Name the snowman and post the name on the bulletin board. Let children write the snowman's name in their journals and draw a picture of it.

Winter String Art Picture

Materials: Two pieces of yarn or string 12"/30 cm in length; dark blue construction paper; white and black tempera paint; two clothespins

Directions: Use two trays (foam meat trays work well); place white paint in one and black in the other.

Child folds paper in half width-wise and then opens it up. Fasten a clothespin to the end of the yarn. Holding the clothespin, dip the yarn in the white paint tray. Child places yarn on one half of the construction paper leaving the clothespin off the paper. Fold the paper over and hold it down firmly with one hand. Use the other hand to pull the string out from between the folded paper. Repeat the procedure with the black paint. Repeat a few times.

Additional Activities: What does the design look like? At the bottom of the picture, write the story that child dictates. Try other colors, heavier string, or different colored construction paper.

Songs and Poetry

Ten Little Snowmen

Tune: "Ten Little Indians"

One little, two little, three little snowmen.
Four little, five little, six little snowmen.
Seven little, eight little, nine little snowmen.
Ten little cheery snowmen.

Winter Is So Very Cold

Tune: "Mary Had A Little Lamb"

Winter is so very cold,
Very cold, very cold.
Winter is so very cold,
With snowflakes falling down.

Watch them as they drift and float,
Drift and float, drift and float.
Watch them as they drift and float,
To the winter ground.

Snowflakes

Tune: "Twinkle, Twinkle, Little Star"

Snowflakes, snowflakes
Twirl around
Snowflakes, snowflakes
Falling down.

Snowflakes, snowflakes
Touch my tongue
Snowflakes, snowflakes
My song is sung.

Snowflakes, snowflakes
Twirl around
Snowflakes, snowflakes
Falling down.

Songs and Poetry *(cont.)*

Snowman

Tune: "The Ensy Weensy Spider"

The great big giant snowman
Sat in our front yard.
Out came the sun and
The snowman melted away.
_____ went to see him
child's name
But he was not there.
And the great big giant snowman
Was never seen again.

Ice Poems

I like ice
Ice skating,
Ice chewing,
Ice sledding,
Ice falling,
OUCH!

It's fun to chew on a slice of ice.
I like ice
It's fun to slide on a slice of ice.
I like ice.
Ice is nice.

Winter Snow

Tune: "What Shall we do with a Drunken Sailor"

The winter snow came down so hard
The winter snow came down so hard
The winter snow came down so hard
Ear—ly in the morning!

Children ran out and threw snowballs
Children ran out and threw snowballs
Children ran out and threw snowballs
Ear—ly in the morning!

Variation: Let the children make up verses; "Children went sledding, skiing, or snow came down so softly, " etc. Use hand actions with the songs.

Movement Activities

Rag Doll Movements

Before doing the winter movements below, let children loosen up by being rag dolls.

To introduce movements, bring a rag doll. Show how rag dolls flop. Have the children work with a partner and practice flopping left leg, right leg, arms, heads. One child helps the other child flop gently.

> **My arms hang loose**
> **My neck hangs down**
> **My legs, are floppy free,**
> **Can you guess who I am?**
> **Why I'm a rag doll,**
> **Can't you see?**

Ask the children to:

> make light runs around in a circle
> bend head until hanging
> hang arms freely
> hang head freely
> loosen and free shoulders

As you demonstrate with a rag doll, ask the children to swing with arms bent, hanging their torsos. Let the swing grow larger and higher. Can the swing take you into a turn? Can the swing let you travel?

Winter Feet

Have the children take off their shoes. Can you feel your feet moving on the carpet? On the floor? Which is colder? Why? Lying down match the soles of your feet with a partner's feet. How does that feel? Roll over together while touching partner's feet and move them up in the air.

Bear Feet

Walk like a bear stalking a rabbit in the snow (soft-quiet).

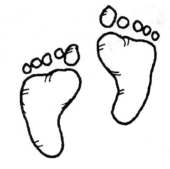

Get a partner. One stalks, and one waits with back turned and eyes closed. The child stalking moves very slowly and quietly and doesn't tap the partner until right up to him/her. Remember how a cat stalks. Be so silent your partner cannot hear you coming.

Go forward, backward, sideways, and around with your bear feet. Now, run like a bear!

Winter Curl

You are very cold. Can you curl up to get warm? Have the children do the following curls: a standing curl, one finger, hands, arms, legs, spine, sideways curl, roll curl, and an uncurl.

       40

Cooking Projects

Snow Cheese Treats

Materials: Cream cheese; small loaf of nut or date bread; plastic knives; fork; bowl; paring knife; raisins; small jellybeans

Directions: Put cream cheese in a bowl and let it sit at room temperature for one hour to soften.

Mash snow (cream cheese) with a fork.

Teacher may cut slices of date or nut bread into quarters (discuss halves and quarters).

Spread snow (cream cheese) on bread in the shape of a circle.

Add jelly beans for eyes and raisins for mouth.

Popcorn Snowman

Materials: Hot plate or electric skillet; wax paper; six cups popped popcorn; 20 marshmallows; 2 tbls./30 mL vegetable shortening; margarine; raisins; jellybeans; heart-shaped cinnamon candies

Directions: Pop corn and set aside. Melt marshmallows and smooth in shortening. Add popcorn, one cup at a time; coat well. Butter hand; mold popcorn into balls and stick together on wax paper to form a snowman. Every five children can form one snowman. Add raisins, candies, and jellybeans for decorations.

Additional Activities: Children can make a construction paper snowman that looks like the popcorn one.

Tell the story of the Gingerbread Boy. What might a Popcorn Boy do? Maybe he could go to Mars or to the moon. Make up a group story and write it on a chart paper as the children tell it. Write the story on individual pages for a Big Book.

My Spring Robin

by Anne Rockwell

Summary

A little girl is remembering the song she heard a robin sing last year. She goes looking for the robin and finds a bee, a toad, early crocuses, daffodils, and earthworms, but no robin. Then she hears something. "Cheer-up, cheerilee!" She has found her spring robin.

This is a perfect book for introducing spring. The illustrations are bright and colorful. The book gives the teacher many spring ideas to explore.

SETTING THE STAGE

Recognizing Robins

Materials: Pictures of robin and two other birds native to your area; index cards

Preparations: Discuss robins. Show a picture of a robin. Display two other bird pictures; i.e., blue jay and meadowlark. Discuss and write the names of the birds on index cards. Let the children match the bird names with the pictures.

Hide the robin picture in the classroom so the children can find it without looking under anything. Then let the children go on a "robin hunt." Teach the children to walk away from the picture without pointing or saying anything and then, after they've moved away, give a signal indicating they have found it. The signal might be touching their ear, nose, head, etc. Children enjoy this game as it helps them become aware of their environment and sharpens their visual skills.

SETTING THE STAGE *(cont.)*

Looking for Signs of Spring

Materials: Tape recorder or paper and pencil on clipboard; chart-paper or chalkboard

We heard...

children yelling . . . .Tom
birds singing . . . . Sue
noise in the grass . . Gail

Preparations: Take a spring listening walk. Take a portable tape recorder and record sounds, or take paper and pencil and list sounds as the children hear them. When you return to the classroom, list on chart paper or chalkboard the sounds each child heard.

ENJOYING THE BOOK

Robin's Sound

Read the book. Discuss what sound the robin made. Can the children make that same sound? Have them try. "Cheer-up, cheerilee!"

If possible, get a recording of a robin singing and let the children listen to it.

Before rereading the book, ask the children to listen for all the names of flowers in the book. Every time they hear a flower name, they can put a finger up.

After reading the book, ask how many types of flowers were in the book.

Reread the page showing the daffodils. Read the poem "Dafodowndilly" by A.A. Milne.

Daffodil Art Project

Materials: Yellow foam egg cartons cut into individual cups—1 cup per child; dark or medium blue construction paper; yellow and green construction paper; scissors; glue

Directions: Cut green stem and leaves and yellow petals; place egg cup in the center. Paste on blue paper.

Hang art work on bulletin board with a copy of the nursery rhyme, "Daffodils."

**Daffy-down-dilly has come to town
In a yellow petticoat and a green gown.**

Book Discussion/Calendar

Discuss the book in more detail. What month was on the calendar? When is the first day of spring? Children fill in the numbers on a March calendar. Circle the first day of spring.

EXTENDING THE BOOK

Spring Flower Book

Materials: Seed or flower catalogs or magazines with pictures of flowers; copies of page 45 (at least one page per student); scissors; glue; pencil

Directions: Print color words and the words "big" and "small" on a blackboard or chart. The child cuts a flower out of a magazine or catalog and glues it onto a copy of page 45. Then the child copies the color of his flower in the first blank and the size in the second blank.

These pages can be compiled into a class book and made available for class check out. If the children want, they can make extra pages to take home or make a small book with several pages of their own.

Variation: For a more challenging exercise, let the child write the sentence and spell the words themselves. They can also make spring books by cutting out and labeling pictures that remind them of spring.

Writing Challenges

These can be discussion questions or used as ideas for paintings at the easel. The child dictates the story or sentence to you and you write it at the bottom of the painting.

1. If you could create a new season, what would it be like?

2. List all the words that remind you of spring.

3. Why are many animal babies born in the spring? What animals are born in the spring?

4. Have you ever played or worked in the mud on a spring day? If so, tell about it. If not, tell what you think it would feel like to go barefoot in the mud.

5. It is spring and a fluffy white cloud picks you up and carries you up over the trees and into the sky. What is it like? Where are you going? What do you see?

6. It is spring and the rain has created a small pond around your house. How will you get out?

Name _____

My Spring Flower

My flower is _____
(color)

and _____
(size)

Language Arts

The Purple Crocus

Material: Purple cellophane or purple tissue

Directions: Gently wad the cellophane or tissue in your hand or let students do this. As you tell the story, slowly release it. It will "grow." The students may also act out the story.

Story:

Once upon a time there was a little purple crocus who lived all alone in a dark house under the ground. One day she heard a tapping at the door. She asked who it was. The answer came back that it was the rain, and he wanted to come into the little crocus' house. He sounded sad, but the little crocus wouldn't invite him in to her dark little house.

So she stayed alone for several hours, when once more there was a rapping, this time at her window. It was the rain just a little more forceful than before. Again he asked to come in, and again the crocus answered, "**NO!**"

It was very still for a while, until there came a soft, swaying kind of sound. The crocus heard this noise and asked who it was. This time it was the sun who answered; like the rain she wanted to come in. But, sadly, the crocus wouldn't let her. The little purple flower continued to sit quietly in her dark house.

By and by she heard the soft, swaying noise and a pounding noise at her door. Looking up she saw both the rain and the sun. Together they asked to be let in. With both of them there the little crocus felt that maybe she had better see what they wanted. She had scarcely opened her door, when both swooped into her little dark house.

Holding her hands, they began to run with her. They ran all the way up to the top of the ground and told her to look through. She did. There she found herself in a beautiful garden along with several other flowers. The little purple crocus was thrilled to be part of the flowers in the garden. As she began to sway softly in the gentle breeze, she silently thanked the sun and the rain for helping her to become part of all the beauty that is springtime.

46

Poetry and Songs

Robin, Bobbin, Bobbin

Tune: "Sing a Song of Sixpence"

**Robin Bobbin Bobbin
Flew up in a tree
Sung a song of Springtime
Just for you and me.**

**Tweedle dum, tweedle dee
Tweedle dum dee dee
Sung a song of Springtime
Just for you and me.**

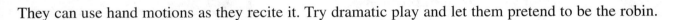

Have students memorize the first verse.

They can use hand motions as they recite it. Try dramatic play and let them pretend to be the robin.

Variations: Replace robin with another bird. Replace spring with another season.

Did You Ever See a Red Bird?

Tune: "Did You Ever See a Lassie?"

**Did you ever see a red bird,
a red bird, a red bird?
Did you ever see a red bird
Sitting in her nest?**

Variations: Change color of bird, type of bird, and activity bird is doing. Let the children make up verses. Write the color words for them to see as they change the song.

Change the song and use the children's names:

**Mary, did you see a red bird,
a red bird, a red bird?
Mary, did you see a red bird,
Sitting in her nest?**

Flowers in the Springtime

**Flowers in the springtime
Yellow, red, and blue
Flowers in the springtime
Waiting just for you.**

Poetry and Songs *(cont.)*

Did You Ever See a Birdhouse?

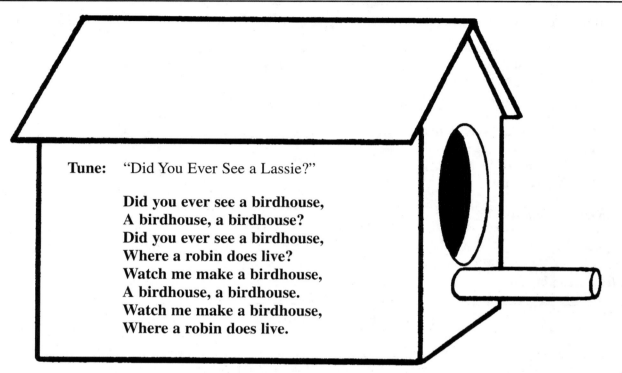

Tune: "Did You Ever See a Lassie?"

Did you ever see a birdhouse,
A birdhouse, a birdhouse?
Did you ever see a birdhouse,
Where a robin does live?
Watch me make a birdhouse,
A birdhouse, a birdhouse.
Watch me make a birdhouse,
Where a robin does live.

(Sing this song while making the birdhouse mobile on page 57 or drawing a birdhouse.)

Spring, Spring, Spring is Here

Tune: "Row, Row, Row, Your Boat"

Spring, spring, spring is here,
Spring is here today.
Sing, sing, sing, a song
For spring is here today.

(This may be done as a round.)

Ten Little Robins

Tune: "Ten Little Indians"

1 little, 2 little, 3 little robins
4 little, 5 little, 6 little robins
7 little, 8 little, 9 little robins
10 little singing robins.

Variations: Make flannel board robins to go along with the song, or let children draw birds to hold up with the song. Use fingers or children to represent the robins. Change the type of bird or use other signs of spring.

Movement

Spring River Run

Review Rag Doll Movements (see Winter Movements Page 40).

Divide the class in half and place them in two corners of the room. If your room is small, take the children to the gym or playground.

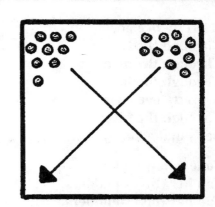

Each group must cross over to the opposite corner of the room without bumping anyone.

Be a fish. Sprint out of the river, flow into the river, and never bump another fish.

Now pretend to be caught in a whirlpool.

Next, be a fish springing out of the water. Combine whirlpool actions and springing actions and move across room without touching any other fish.

Bouncing a Spring Ball

Have children seated on the floor in a circle.

Close your eyes and visualize a ball in your tummy. "What color is it?" "Is it beginning to bounce?" It takes a little bounce at first and then slowly bounces you to your feet. Now it travels and turns with the bouncing. Next let your bounce take you into the air. Can it bounce you back to your seat?

Spring into Spring

Discuss the two types of spring.

Spring up with your feet. Watch your foot work as it leaves the floor. Remember the way a cat springs.

Bend your knees before springing and when landing.

Let your toes come down first.

Practice little springs with soft landings.

Practice five different ways to spring:

> **two feet-2 to 2**
> **two feet-2 to 1 (Come down on one foot)**
> **one foot-1 to 1 (Come down on same foot)**
> **one foot-1 to the other foot (Back and forth)**
> **one foot-1 to 2**

Dance

Pretty Bee

A pretty bee goes
Through the hive,
Through the hive,
Through the hive.
A pretty bee goes
Through the hive.
Let's make honey!

Take a bow and
Tap her (his) shoulders,
Tap her (his) shoulders,
Tap her (his) shoulders.
Take a bow and
Tap her (his) shoulders.
Let's make honey!

The pretty bees go
Off to flowers,
Off to flowers.
The pretty bees go
Off to flowers.
Let's make honey!

Tune: "London Bridge is Falling Down"

Children form circle holding hands. One child is the pretty bee and goes in and out of the hive. When they sing "Let's make honey," all drop hands and snap fingers. The pretty bee stops in front of one child and bows and taps him or her on the shoulder. That child follows the leader in and out of the hive. The first two verses are sung over and over until the game is ended.

(When all children are pretty bees or when you want to end the game, sing this part.)

50

Spring Math Activities

	Robin Greater Than-Less Than

Materials: Duplicate the gameboard (page 52) and a set of number cards (page 53) for each player. Color, laminate, and cut out.

Directions: For student playing alone: Shuffle number cards, and place them in a stack with the numbers facing down. Lay the gameboard in front of you. Take one card at a time from the stack. First play the robin on the upper left. If the number on your card is greater than the robin's number, you win the card. Put it in your pile. If the robin's number is greater, put the card on the robin's pile. Next play the second robin, and so on. After the cards are all gone, count to see who won—you or the robin.

Variations: *For two players:* Use two sets of number cards and one gameboard. Children take turns drawing number cards. The child keeps the card if it's greater than the robin's. If not he puts the card in the robin's pile. Both children discard to this pile. When all cards are gone, count to see who won.

Try playing the game with or without a partner and keep only numbers that are less than the robin's numbers.

Spring Rain Problem Solving—Estimation

Materials: Eyedropper; thimble; water

Directions: Students estimate the number of drops it will take until water spills over the side of a thimble. Record estimations on chalkboard or chart paper. As you drop the water into the thimble, have the students count with you. Stop when thimble is half full, and let the students tell you which guesses are too low or too high. Cross these out. Continue putting in drops until water spills over. Check the chart. Which numbers were the closest?

Robin Egg Addition/Subtraction

Materials: One egg carton per child; twelve counters to represent eggs per child (beans, seeds, buttons, etc.)

Directions: Give each child an egg carton and twelve counters. Discuss top row, bottom row, left side, and right side.

Have the child place one counter in each egg cup on the top row. How many eggs did you put in? How many egg cups are in each row? Starting on the left side, add one counter in the first cup on the bottom row. How many altogether now? (You can write the equations on the board; $6 + 1 = 7$) If you take that one out, how many will be left in the egg carton? Continue adding and subtracting with the "eggs."

Variation: Children write equations as they add and subtract eggs.

Robin Greater Than—Less Than Game

Your Cards

2

5

3

7

Robin's Cards

Numbers Cards

Use with Robin Greater Than—Less Than Game.

See page 51 for directions.

6		12	
5		11	
4		10	
3		9	
2		8	
1		7	

Science

Stick Puppet Rain Story

The Story of Ryan Raindrop

Materials: Stick puppets

Preparation: Reproduce patterns on pages 54 and 55. Make enough raindrops so each child will have a puppet. Color, write names on back of each item, laminate, and cut them out. Tape to craft sticks.

Directions: Distribute the stick puppets and tell the following story.

Once upon a time a teeny-tiny raindrop fell upon a green leaf. (Children hold up Ryan Raindrop and leaf.) It stayed on the leaf until the sun came out. (Hold up sun.) The sun warmed the little raindrop and it changed into vapor. The vapor mixed with the air, and we could no longer see it. (Take away raindrop and leaf.) The air then cooled the vapor and it changed back into a raindrop. (Bring back raindrop.) The tiny raindrop found other raindrops, and when they all got together they formed a cloud. (All raindrops join together and go behind cloud and hover above the earth.) There were so many raindrops in the cloud that they began to fall and come back to earth again. (Raindrops fall out of cloud and cloud goes away.) One even fell on the same green leaf! And that's the story of rain.

Variations: Put stick puppets in dramatic play center, and let children retell the story on their own.

Let children make their own set of stick puppets.

Retell the story, letting the children tell you which part comes next.

Rain Puppet Patterns

Science and Art

Making Rain

Materials: Hot plate or electric skillet; tea kettle or pan filled with water; ice cubes; pie pan or flat cake pan

Directions: Boil water and let steam rise. Discuss vapor. Put ice cubes in the pie pan. Let children feel the bottom of the pan. (It will be cold.) Now hold the pan about ten to twelve inches over the steam. Ask the children to look at the bottom of the pan and see what is forming. (Little drops of water will form.) When these drops get heavy enough they will fall like rain. Let the children feel the moisture on the bottom of the pan. What is happening? Why does this happen? Do you think this happens outside when it's raining?

Information: Clouds form as water vapor in the air cools, condenses, and changes to tiny drops of liquid water. When these droplets become so heavy and large that the cloud cannot hold them, they may fall to the earth. We call it rain if they appear as drops of water.

Magnolia Trees

Materials: Blue construction paper; brown paint, crayon or chalk; pink and white paint; green and yellow felt tip pens

Directions: Have the children draw a bare tree and branches with brown paint, crayon, or chalk. Let dry.

Dip pointer finger in white paint and touch ends of branches to make magnolia blossoms. Let this dry (child may blow it dry). Dip little finger in pink paint to touch base of white blossoms. Add green leaves with felt tip markers. With a yellow marker, add a touch of yellow to the center of each blossom.

Science and Art *(cont.)*

Birdhouse Mobile

Materials: Brown lunch bags; sticks or twigs; range and brown construction paper; tagboard patterns (page 58); string or yarn; hole punch; scissors; crayons or felt tip pens; stapler; paste or glue

Preparations: For each child cut a 3 inch circle near the bottom of one side of a lunch bag. Give each child a 9" x 12" (22.5 x 30 cm) piece of brown construction paper and a 3" x 6" (8 x 15 cm) piece of orange paper. Each child will also need three 12" (30 cm) pieces of string.

Directions: Child traces one bird and two wing patterns on brown paper and two breasts on orange paper. Add eyes and beak with crayons or pens. Cut out. Paste orange breasts and staple wings on each side of bird. Fold down opening of paper bag approximately one inch and staple shut. While still folded, use crayons to decorate paper bag birdhouse. Puff bag out through hole. Punch one hole in the center of the top of the bag and one hole in center of the bird. Tie string to the bird and the other end to the twig. Tie one string to the paper bag and the other end to the twig to make a mobile. Use the third string to hang up the mobile. Tie it on both ends of the twig and balance it. Hang the mobiles up and enjoy them!

Variations: Children may want to make a nest and eggs in the birdhouse. Use scrap paper to make eggs and either tear paper or collect grass, etc. for the nest from the school grounds. They can also add legs to the robin.

You can use any color for the bird. If you are talking about your state bird, use those colors.

You might want to label the parts of the mobile; i.e. bird, birdhouse, nest, etc. The child can write the words or copies of the words could be made available for the child to cut and paste on the correct item.

Have the children sing the song "Did You Ever See a Birdhouse?" on page 48, while they work on their birdhouses.

Science and Art *(cont.)*

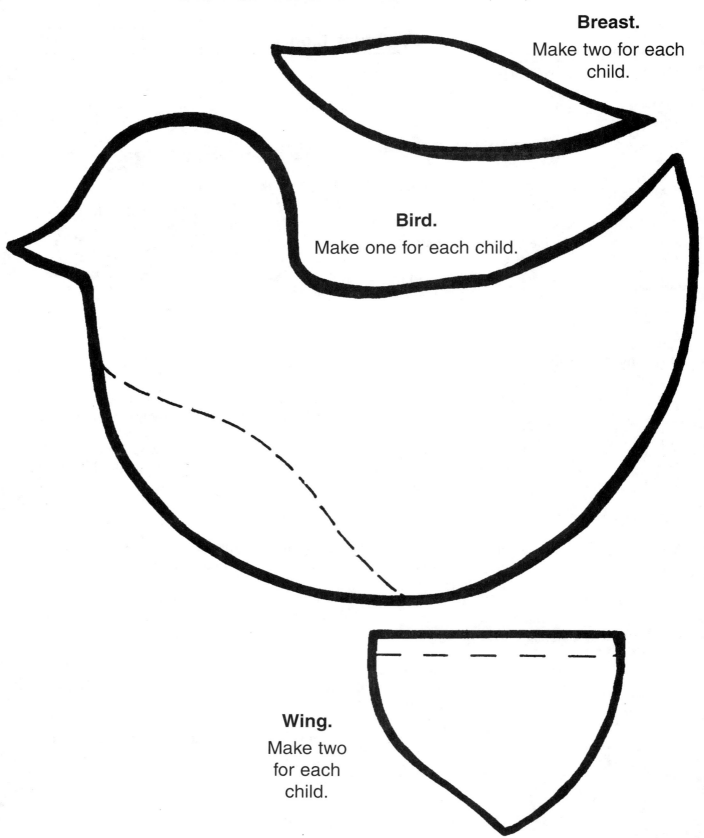

Breast.
Make two for each child.

Bird.
Make one for each child.

Wing.
Make two for each child.

58

Food Activities

Mud Pudding

Materials: Instant chocolate pudding and items necessary to make it; one coated paper plate per child or wax paper; spoon

Directions: Get a copy of the poem "Mud" by Polly Boyden found in *Read-Aloud Rhymes for the Very Young* selected by Jack Prelutsky, page 13. Read it to the children. Have children help make the pudding and give each 2 to 3 spoonfuls on the plate or wax paper. The children can play in the "mud" with their fingers and eat the pudding.

Variation: Fingerpaint with pudding on finger paint paper and let dry.

Toasted Bird Bread

Materials: Toaster; bread; knives; jam, butter or margarine

Directions: Discuss spring birds and what they might like to eat. Could you make a piece of toast and put jam on in the shape of a bird or a nest? Try it. What does it look like?

Variation: On the bottom of a piece of paper write what shape each child made with his/her jam. The children can illustrate their papers. Turn them upside down. What do they look like now? Write on that side of the paper.

Marshmallow Birds

Materials: Marshmallows; round candy; candy corn; round toothpicks; canned frosting

Directions: Use toothpicks for legs. Attach candy eyes and candy corn beak with the canned frosting to the marshmallow body.

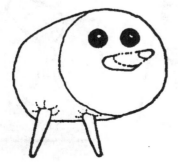 

Time of Wonder

by Robert McCloskey

Summary

A family experiences summertime on the coast of Maine. They enjoy all the wonderful sights which include the ocean, a summer storm, fog, a variety of boats, different types of birds and fish, and a seaplane. Then the family prepares for and lives through a hurricane. After the storm, they explore the damage the hurricane has caused.

This is an excellent book for introducing summer. Children will enjoy the beautifully descriptive text and distinctive watercolor illustrations.

SETTING THE STAGE

Summer Discussion

Materials: Index cards; pocket chart or bulletin board; HEADINGS — Summer, Fall, Winter, Spring, written on strips of construction paper

Directions: Have a class discussion about summer. Ask the children to tell what they like to do in the summer. As they dictate sentences to you, write them on the index cards. Have them post their index cards under the SUMMER heading on the pocket chart of bulletin board.

Colored Sand Picture

Materials: Sand; resealable plastic bags, one for each color; food coloring; poster board; glue

Directions: Pour some sand into several resealable plastic bags. Add a few drops of food coloring to each. Seal the bags. Shake until the color mixes evenly in the sand. Open the bags. Let the sand dry for a couple of hours. Have each child plan a picture so he or she will know where to put each color. Smear glue on the areas where a particular color of sand should go. Sprinkle the sand onto the glue. Allow the glue to dry. Gently shake off any excess sand. Repeat for each color of sand until the picture is complete.

Variations:

1. Combine the sand colors and mix them only slightly. Shaking the sand onto the picture will give a rainbow effect.
2. Make layered sand designs in bottles with the remaining colored sand. Use interestingly shaped bottles and tilt them in different directions to create a variety of designs.

ENJOYING THE BOOK

Sailboat

Materials: Light-weight paper plate; pencil; scissors; markers

Directions: Fold the paper plate in half and then unfold it. Draw a boat design with the mast and sail above the fold line and the top of the boat on the fold line. Cut around the mast and sail. Fold the plate again, using the original fold line to bring the mast and sail up. Use markers to color the waves, boat, and sail.

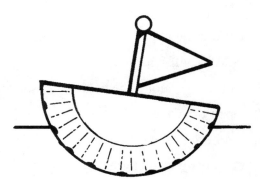

Variations:

1. For sparkling waves, add glue and glitter to the colored wavy lines.
2. Glue on fish-shaped crackers so it will look like there are fish in the ocean.
3. Personalize each boat by writing the child's name on the side. Invite the children to pick their favorite numbers and write them on the sails.

Sea Picture

Materials: Watercolors; watercolor paintbrushes; plastic cup; water; old ruler, mixing stick, or craft stick; watercolor or other white paper; crayons; paper towels; plastic tablecloth

Directions: Have the children make underwater pictures using white paper and crayons. Be sure they do not to use crayon to color in the water parts of the picture. After the pictures are done, make a blue watercolor wash. Do this by adding water to blue watercolor paint in a cup. Mix the paint with an old ruler, mixing stick, or craft stick. The mixture should leave a blue tint when applied to the paper. Let the children use paintbrushes to apply this blue watercolor wash over their pictures. The crayon sections will not hold the watercolor.

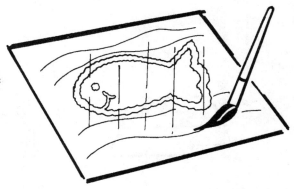

Origami Fan

Materials: One rectangular piece of paper, measuring 5" x 15" (13 cm x 38 cm), for each child; stapler (optional)

Directions: Place the rectangle on a table or desk so that the longer side is horizontal. Fold the paper in half from side to side. Continue to fold it in half from side to side three more times. Unfold the paper. Crease the lines to make alternating up and down folds. Pinch one end of the fan together and fold it up slightly. You may wish to staple this end in place. Gently pull on the sides of the other end to spread the fan.

ENJOYING THE BOOK *(cont.)*

Little Book

Materials: One copy of little book (page 63) for each student; crayons

Preparation:

1. Fold page 63 in half lengthwise, after cutting along dashed lines.
2. Fold in half again.
3. Fold in half again.
4. Unfold the paper. (You should have eight parts now.)
5. Fold in half width-wise.
6. Cut or tear along the center crease from the folded edge to the dot. (See diagram below.)
7. Open the paper.
8. Fold it lengthwise again.
9. Push the end sections together to fold into a little book. Four pages will be formed.

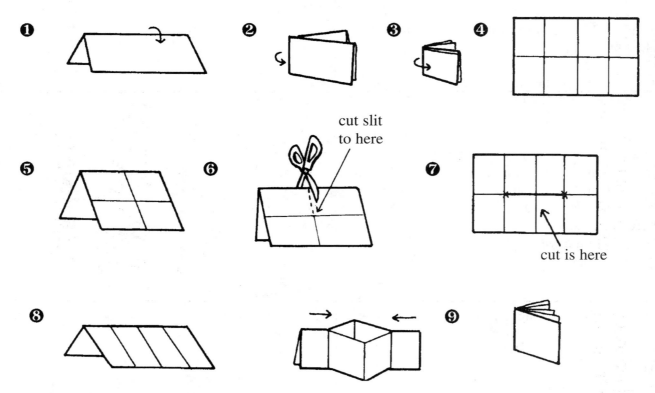

Directions:

After the children have folded and illustrated the book, let them take turns reading it to you or reading it together in a group. Let them find and read to a partner. Bring in older students, parent volunteers, or aides to listen to the books. When the children have worked with the book for a day or two, let them take it home to read to their parents.

Little Book *(cont.)*

I like to smell _____ .

I like to eat _____ .

The thing I like least about summer is _____ .

The thing I like most about summer is _____ .

During the summer, I like to watch _____ .

When summer ends, I will _____ .

SUMMER

by _____

I like to hear _____ .

EXTENDING THE BOOK

The Sun—Discussion

Read Aesop's fable "The North Wind and the Sun." If possible, get a copy with illustrations. (See Bibliography, page 80, for a suggested version.) After reading, ask the following questions: Who won the argument? Why? Is this a true story? How do you know that the sun is warm?

Picture Box Writing

Materials: A shoe box; index cards; pictures of summer items; glue

Preparation: Find pictures of summer items such as watermelon, swimming, corn on the cob, beach umbrella, patio furniture, etc. Glue each to an index card and write its name on the card. Store cards in shoe box.

Directions: Children draw cards out of the box and write a sentence using that word, or simply copy the word on the card. They can also use this for a guessing game. The child draws a card out of the box and describes it to the other children. They must guess what he/she is describing.

Writing Challenges

Use these sentence starters to challenge students.

1. When summer comes I want to…
2. When summer comes I will go to…
3. I wish I could go to…
4. The thing I like best about summer is…
5. When it's hot, I like to…
6. If I were a fish, I would…
7. I like to play in water because…

Word Stamps

Materials: Wooden stamps with words on them-e.g., that, and, is, this, good, I, you, etc. (available in teacher supply stores); index cards; pencil or pen

Directions: The child writes sentences with the stamps. They may add words or sentences having to do with summer with a pen or pencil. These can be illustrated and even made into small individual books.

Math Activities

Spot the Frog

Materials: One frog (page 66) and one set of blank spots (page 67) for every two players.

Preparation: Put numerals in the circles on the frog. Color and laminate frogs and spots. Cut out. In place of spots, counters, buttons, etc. could be used.

Directions: Cover each number with a spot so that the number does not show. The children take turns uncovering the numbers. If they can name the number, they keep the spot. If not, they put the spot back on the frog. The child with the most spots is the winner.

Variations: Write equations on the frog, and the child must give the correct answer after removing the spot.
Or, write the answers on the circles, and the child must match the correct circle to the correct spot on the frog. This can be used for letters and sounds, also.

Watermelon Math

Materials: Duplicate one watermelon per child on page 68; scissors; red, green, and black crayons

Directions: 1. Child cuts out and colors the watermelon red, and the rind green.

2. On the line on the right side the child writes a number up to 20.

3. The child then draws the same number of black seeds on the red part of the watermelon.

Variation: Glue on black buttons for seeds or use a hole punch and punch holes out of black construction paper for seeds.

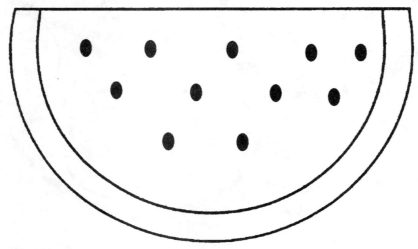

         #251 Seasons

Spot the Frog

Spot the Frog *(cont.)*

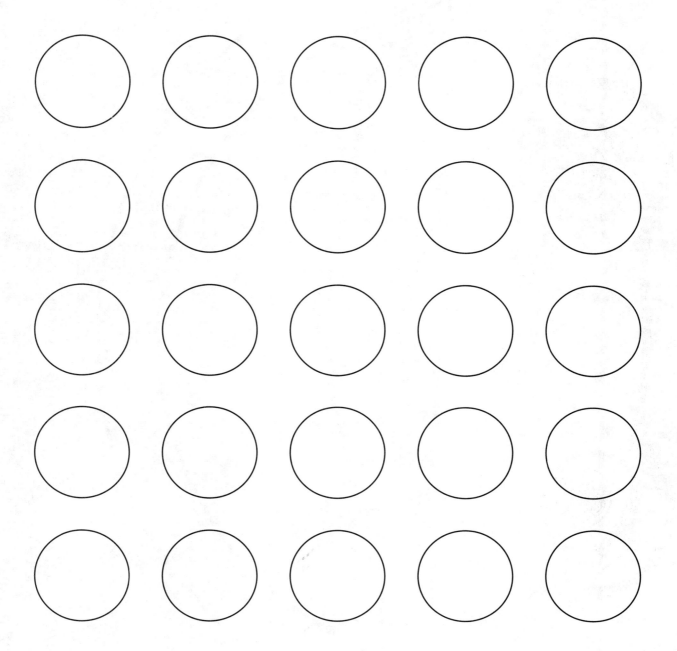

Watermelon Math

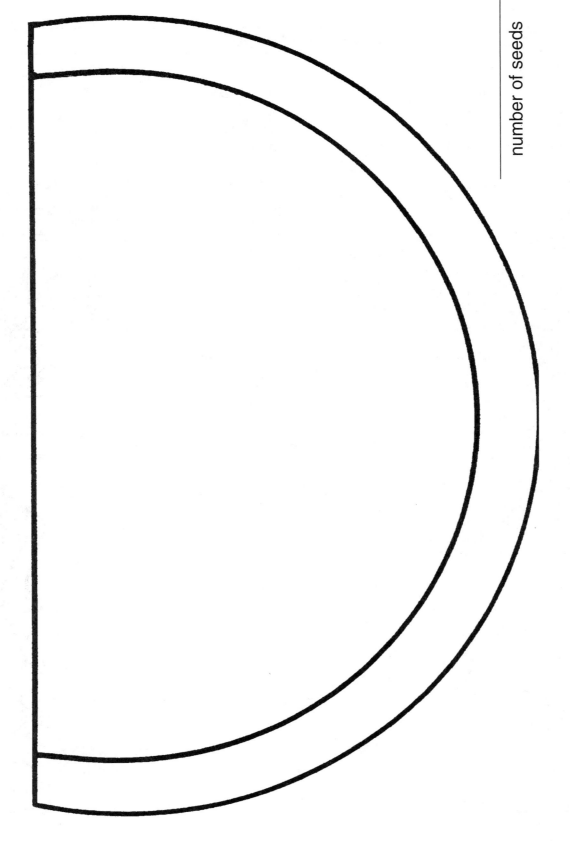

number of seeds

1. Color the watermelon red.

2. Color the rind green.

3. Write a number on the line up to 20.

4. Use a black crayon to draw the number of seeds on the red.

Summer Songs

Goodnight Tadpole

Tune: "Goodnight Ladies"

Goodnight Tadpole	**Good Morning, Frog.**
Goodnight Tadpole	**Good Morning, Frog.**
Goodnight Tadpole	**Good Morning, Frog.**
I'll see you in the morn'.	**Where did your tail go?**

Variations: Add a third verse, "Where did you get your feet?"

Summer Frogs

Tune: "Frere Jacques" ("Are You Sleeping?")

Big frogs, little frogs, fat frogs, thin frogs,
Leaping frogs, sleeping frogs,
Swimming frogs and tadpoles,
Listen to the frogs croak,

Croak—Croak—PEEP
Croak—Croak—PEEP

GR-R-UMP!

A Child Had a Little Frog

Tune: "Mary had a Little Lamb"

_____ had a tadpole,
"Child's name"

a tadpole, a tadpole.

_____ , had a tadpole,
"Child's name"

It's tail was long and brown.

_____ had a little frog,
"Child's name"

Little frog, little frog.

_____ had a little frog,
"Child's name"

It's legs were green and long.

Variations: Change frogs to flowers, fruits, fish, birds, etc.

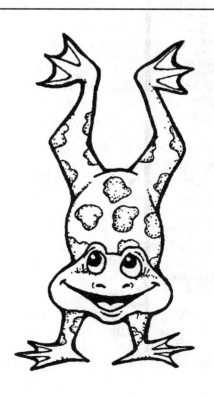

Summer Science

Flannel Board Story

Materials: Flannel board, props (patterns are on pages 71 and 72)

Preparation: See directions, page 71, for making flannel board props.

Directions: Using the props, tell the following story to children.

Sheryl and the Sun

Sheryl was a little girl who was bored one day. She decided to put on her coat and go outside to play. (Put Sheryl on flannelboard and put coat on Sheryl. Add horizon and tree.) It was a beautiful day with the sun shining high in the sky. (Add sun, short tree shadow, and short girl shadow.)

Sheryl noticed her shadow and had fun trying to run away from it. Sometimes she was able to hide it in the tree's shadow. She played for a very long time. She became so hot that she took off her coat. Then she noticed that while she had been playing, the sun had moved to another part of the sky. (Lower sun.) She saw that her shadow had grown very long and so had the tree's shadow. (Exchange shadows.)

Then a fluffy white cloud blew slowly across the sky covering the sun. (Move cloud across sky and cover the sun.) Sheryl couldn't see the sun any more. (Take away shadows.) Sheryl noticed that her shadow and the tree's had disappeared. She also began to feel chilly so she put her coat back on. (Put on coat.)

It was starting to get dark, so Sheryl decided she had better go. (Lower sun and remove Sheryl.) Her day had been a lot of fun and she had learned a lot about the sun.

Discussion: How do we know the sun is hot? When do things outside have shadows? Why are shadows sometimes short and sometimes long? What happened when the clouds went in front of the sun? Why did the air get cooler when the sun set? When the sun is high in the sky, do you have breakfast, lunch, or dinner? If it is cloudy, where is the sun?

Variations: Retell the story and let the children place the characters on the flannel board. As you remove the characters, let the children tell you which one was put on first, second, etc.

Flannel Board Props

Directions:

1. Reproduce props on pages 71 and 72 onto heavy paper or trace onto felt or interfacing.

2. If using paper, color, laminate, and cut out. Glue or staple a strip of felt or interfacing to the back of each prop.

3. If using felt or interfacing, decorate with permanent marking pens.

Example

Cut a 3"/8 cm width for horizon.

Flannel Board
Props *(cont.)*

72

Summer

Science

| **Air Conditioner Experiment** |

Materials: Bowl of ice cubes; electric fan

Directions: Let children take turns standing in front of the fan. Now set up the electric fan so that air blows across the ice cubes. Let the children take turns standing in the cool air. Can they feel a difference?

Variation: Blindfold the children and let them stand in front of fan with and without ice cubes. Can they tell whether the ice cubes are there or not?

Preparation: Explain that an air conditioner sends warm air across tubes that are filled with a cold liquid. Ask what happens to the air as it crosses the cold tubes.

| **Shadow Experiences** |

Chalk Shadows

Materials: Chalk (wide stick is best, but chalkboard chalk will work, too); a sunny day!

Directions: Take children outside and let them outline the shadow of the school at different times during the day. Let them stand in a certain spot and have a partner outline their shadow. Go out later and note the changes in the shadows. Where are shadows now? Are they opposite the sun? What direction does the sun rise in? Where does it move as it goes through the sky? Which direction does it set in?

Shadow Play

Materials: Overhead projector or movie projector; screen or blank wall

Directions: Let the children take turns making shadows in front of the light.

Shadow Friend

Materials: Poem, "My Shadow" by Robert Lewis Stevenson from *A Child's Garden of Verses*, Franklin Watts, 1966.

Directions: Let the children choose partners. One child will need to be the shadow. As the teacher reads the poem, the children will move as people and shadows. Take turns being person or shadow.

Variation: Turn out the lights and read the poem again. Encourage them to try to fool their shadow. Let them experiment.

Shadow Experiences *(cont.)*

My Shadow

Materials: Copies of the sun, child, and the child's shadow from page 72 (one set per child); scissors; glue; 12" x 18"/30 x 45 cm sheet of light blue construction paper, one per child

Directions: Children color, cut out, and paste objects on blue paper. Watch to make sure they place the sun, shadow, and child correctly. Discuss.

Shadow Games

Shadow Tag

Materials: A bright sunny day!

Directions: Go outside on a sunny day and play shadow tag. One child is "It" and tries to "tag" another child by stepping on his/her shadow. That child then becomes "It."

Variations: When "It" steps on someone else's shadow, they both become "It," and everyone continues stepping on shadows until everyone is "It."

Simon Says Shadow Game

Materials: A bright sunny day!

Directions: Play the same as "Simon Says," only ask the shadow to do the activities. For instance, "Simon's shadow says make your shadow dance, Simon's shadow says make your shadow hop, Simon's shadow says sit down," etc.

Shadow Poems

Read-Aloud Rhymes for the Very Young selected by Jack Prelutsky and illustrated by Marc Brown is a delightful collection of children's poetry covering a wide variety of topics. On page 25 there are three charming poems that will enhance your study of shadows. They are: "Hide-and-Seek Shadow" by Margaret Hillert, "Poor Shadow" by Ilo Orleans, and "Look" by Charlotte Zolotow.

74

Art Activities

Frog Art

Materials: Paper plates; green paint or green crayons; scissors; felt pens; stapler

Directions: Paint or color back side of plate green. Let dry. Child will draw two half circles at the bottom of the plates and cut out. These will be the eyes.

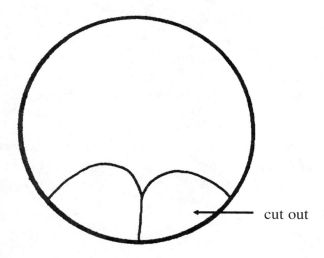

cut out

With a felt pen draw a half circle at the top of each eye. Color it black or leave it outlined. Staple to the top of the plate. Add mouth and nostrils with pens.

Summer Sun Art

Materials: Large paper; scissors; paint

Directions: Cut a circular hole in the upper half of paper. The child paints a picture around the hole. The hole can be used as the sun, the center of a flower, or anything else they can imagine. Write at the bottom of the painting what the child painted.

Variation: Have yellow (and other colors) tissue paper available. Child can paste tissue paper in back of the hole for sun or the center of a flower, etc., when they have finished the painting.

Culminating Activity

Summer Vegetable Tasting Party

Materials: Letter to parents (page 77; ask one parent to send a vegetable dip); copies of vegetable tasting sheet (page 77, one per student); electric skillet, wok or hot plate with frying pan; oil for frying; small paper plates, forks, napkins (you can ask parents to supply the last four items)

Preparations: Ask for parent help the day of the party. Let the children help clean and prepare the vegetables.

Directions: Cook some of each vegetable. Encourage the children to taste each vegetable when it's raw and when it's cooked. They may use the dip if they wish. Then they record on the taster's rating sheets a happy face if they liked it, and a sad face if they didn't, or write YES or NO in the spaces.

Follow Up Activity: Discuss and compare tasters' sheets. Did they have more happy faces or sad faces? Did they like more raw vegetables or cooked vegetables? Did they taste anything they'd never tasted before? Was there anything they didn't think they'd like, but did like?

Variations:

1. Save some vegetables and make vegetable prints.

2. Invite another class in to taste vegetables with you or invite in administrators and office staff.

3. Call a local newspaper and invite them to join you.

4. For healthier eating, steam the vegetables instead of frying.

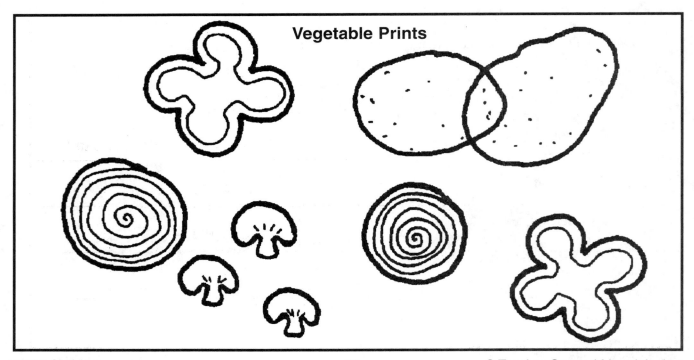

Vegetable Prints

Request Letter/Taster's Rating Sheet

Dear Parents,

You are invited to join us for a summer vegetable tasting party on _____ at

_____ . We are excited about tasting a variety of summertime vegetables, both raw and cooked.

Your child will need to bring some fresh _____ .

Please send it on _____ . If you can't send any, please let me know.

We look forward to seeing you at our party.

Sincerely,

_____
Teacher

Name _____

☺ —Yes, I liked it.   ☹ —No, I didn't like it.

TASTER'S RATING SHEET

Vegetables Tasted	Raw	Cooked
1.		
2.		
3.		
4.		

SUNSHINE AWARD

Name
_____

**Is The Reason
For A Happy Season.
You've Done An Outstanding Job!**

Teacher
_____

Date
_____

Stationery

#251 Seasons

Bibliography

BOOKS

Andrews, Jan. *Very Last First Time.* Antheneum, 1986.

Asch, Frank. *Mooncake.* Prentice-Hall, 1983.

Brett, Jan. *The Mitten.* Putnam, 1989.

Burton, Virginia Lee. *The Little House.* Houghton Mifflin, 1942.

Maestro, Betty & Giulio. *Through the Year With Harriet.* Crown, 1985.

Martin, Charles E. *Island Winter.* Greenwillow, 1984.

Parnall, Peter. *Winter Barn.* Macmillan, 1986.

Pittman, Helen Clare. *The Gift of the Willows.* Carolrhoda, 1988.

Rockwell, Anne. *First Comes Spring.* Crowell, 1985.

Rylant, Cynthia. *This Year's Garden.* Bradbury Press, 1984.

Rylant, Cynthia. *Henry and Mudge in the Green Time.* Bradbury Press, 1987.

Steig, William. *Sylvester and the Magic Pebble.* Scholastic, 1969.

Tresselt, Alvin. *Hi, Mister Robin!* Lothrop, 1955.

Tresselt, Alvin. *It's Time Now!* Lothrop, 1969.

Wells, Rosemary. *Forest of Dreams.* Dial, 1988.

White, Anne Terry (Retold by). *Aesop's Fables.* Random House, 1964.

Yashima, Taro. *Umbrella.* Viking, 1958.

Zolotow, Charlotte. *Over and Over.* Harper & Row, 1957.

POETRY

Brewton, Sara & John E. *Sing a Song of Seasons.* Macmillan, 1955.

Esbensen, Barbara Juster. *Swing Around the Sun.* Lerner, 1971.

Frank, Josette. *Poems to Read to the Very Young.* Random House, 1982.

Hopkins, Lee Bennett (Selected by). *Surprises.* Harper & Row, 1984.

Lewis, Richard (Edited by). *In a Spring Garden.* Dial, 1965.

Stevenson, Robert Lewis. *A Child's Garden of Verses.* "My Shadow." Franklin Watts, 1966.

TECHNOLOGY

Fall Brings Changes; Spring Brings Changes. (Videodiscs); Charles Clark Co., Inc., 4540 Preslyn Drive, Raleigh, NC 27616-3177; 1-800-247-7009.

Seasons by Catherine Slonecki. (Video); 33 min. Educational Activities, Inc., P.O. Box 392, Freeport, NY 11520; 1-800-645-3739 (In NY 516-223-4666).

Seasons by National Geographic Society. (CD-ROM for MAC or WIN); Available from Bound to Stay Bound Books, Inc., 1880 West Morton, Jacksonville, IL 62650. 1-800-637-6586.

Spring Songs That Tickle Your Funny Bone. (Cassette or LP, Songbook, and Activity Guide); Educational Record Center, Inc., 3233 Burnt Mill Drive, Suite 100, Wilmington, NC 28403-2655; 1-800-438-1637.